Written & illustrated by Phillip Reed
(info@phillipreed.net)

website - phillipreed.net

instagram - the_phillustrator

facebook - ThePhillustrator

THE CHRISTMAS LIST

WRITTEN & ILLUSTRATED BY PHILLIP REED

A GIFT BOOK FOR CHILDREN & ADULTS

This book is dedicated to my Mum, Aaron, Mia, Amber and Kelly. Thank you for your support and putting up with me during the writing of this book. x

Dear Reader,

Thank you for choosing to read my book.

This isn't a children's book in the normal sense. Instead, I have written it for all ages, at a time when we are going through one of the greatest challenges we have had to face in living memory. I hope this book can bring you even the smallest of comforts.

This book combines some musings for the season, my love of illustration (especially of cute characters), and the beautiful locations of Manningtree & Mistley, in Essex, UK.

If you feel that you gain something from this book, I would love to to hear from you, so please let me know on social media, or you can email me at info@phillipreed.net.

I hope you enjoy it!

Phillip Reed

Dear Santa,

As a hedgehog I am supposed to be hibernating right now,
but I am too excited about Christmas to sleep.
Instead, I thought I would write my Christmas List.

So here it is:
1. Worms
2. More worms ...??

It isn't a very long list, is it!

I couldn't think of anything else to add, so I went to see my friend Badger to ask him
what he would put on his Christmas list.

"The first thing I would add is COMPANY," he said, giving me a big hug, "There is nothing more
important than being with your friends and family at Christmas."

"But we need to find more ideas," he said, grabbing his scarf. "Let's go for a walk.
I always happen upon my best ideas while I'm out walking."

I thought for a second and remarked, "To find ideas, which is the best way to go?"

"Forward," said Badger.

As we walked, the sun began to rise, and Badger said,

"The second thing I would add to my Christmas list is HOPE because the hope of a new day gets us through the darkest of nights."

I understood this one because I always hope tomorrow will be Christmas Day, and once a year, I am always right.

Mistley Towers - Two porticoed classical towers, which stood at each end of a grandiose but highly unconventional Georgian church, designed by Robert Adam in 1776.(src. english-heritage.org.uk)

"Something I like to do every Christmas is to REFLECT, by taking time to think about everything that has happened and all I have seen and done during the year.

"You can only recognise your face in a reflection once the ripples in the water have stopped."

The Swan Basin (fountain) was commissioned in the 1770s by local politician Richard Rigby, and designed by the Adam brothers, Robert and James. designed by Robert Adam in 1776.(src. www.harwichandmanningtreestandard.co.uk/)

We stopped to give old Mr Mole a Christmas card.

"Loneliness can feel as bitter as a Winter chill," said Badger.

"If you remember someone who spends Christmas alone,
and give them the gift of your time,
it can warm their heart, as well as your own.

So I would add INCLUDE OTHERS to my list."

As we walked through the woods, we came across a tree
where someone had tied a rope to it to use a swing. With a large grin,
Badger grabbed the rope and began swinging back and forth.

"Whatever your age, and however busy you are, make sure that there's
always enough SMILES and SILLINESS to go around at Christmas." he said, laughing.

This swing and tree can be found at Furze Hill Woodland in Mistley, Essex

"Badger, don't you want any nice things for Christmas," I said, "Owning lots of nice things seems to make people happy, that's why they take photos of them to show their friends."

"Nobody can own the nicest of things," said Badger admiring the tree called Old Knobbley*, "and are these people trying to convince their friends that they are happy or themselves?"

"The next thing on my list is to be THANKFUL."

"Remember that you might not have everything that you want, but you probably have everything that you need."

*Old Knobbley is a much loved 800 year old English Oak Tree growing in Mistley, England. With a trunk circumference of about 9.5m and just 4.3m high, (src. www.oldknobbley.co.uk)

"A life well-lived is full of experiences, not belongings. MEMORIES is next on my list. they cost nothing but are a priceless gift that lasts a lifetime."

"Just make sure you are making good ones all the time."

Location - The Walls, Manningtree, overlooking the River Stour.

"The wonderful thing about performing ACTS OF KINDNESS
is that the more that you do,
the happier you feel,
and the happier you feel,
the more you do,"
said Badger.

"The last thing on my Christmas List is SHARING," said Badger.
"Regardless of how much or little that you might have,
you will always have something to offer.
Even if it is just a smile, friendship,
or cups of hot chocolate,
to warm us both up when we get home."

So as you can see I have quite the Christmas list now, but none of them can be found under the tree.

C - COMPANY

H - HOPE

R - REFLECT

I - INCLUDE OTHERS

S - SMILES, SILLINESS (& SWINGS)

T - THANKFUL

M - MEMORIES

A - ACTS OF KINDNESS

S - SHARING

Also, the beauty of them all is that they cost nothing,
we just need to remember that we are already carrying them in our hearts.

Yours sincerely,

Hedgehog

P.S. I would still like some worms though please.

THANK YOU...!!
I really appreciate you reading my book and I hope you enjoyed it.

If you did, please consider leaving a review on amazon to let other readers know about it.

AUTHOR & ILLUSTRATOR *Phillip Reed*

If you like this story you may enjoy Wild Woolly: A rhyming picture book about anti-bullying, kindness and manners

available at
amazon

I wish I had taken a photo of all the children's faces when I read it to my class, they loved it!" – Sally, primary school teacher ★★★★★

You can find out more about me and my other books at my website phillipreed.net

Printed in Great Britain
by Amazon